©1993 text & design PRC Publishing Ltd
©1993 photographs Paddy Cutts/Animals Unlimited

This edition published in 1998 by PRC Publishing Ltd
Kiln House, 210 New Kings Road, London SW6 4NZ
exclusively for SelectaBook Ltd, Folly Road,
Roundway, Devizes, Wiltshire SN10 2HR

© 1998 PRC Publishing Ltd

ISBN 1 85648 156 5

Printed and bound in Singapore

CATS

A Comprehensive Guide to the World's Breeds

PADDY CUTTS

SELECT
EDITIONS

ACKNOWLEDGMENTS

There are many people who have helped with the production of this book, and to whom all due credit must be given.

LARRY JOHNSON, who has supplied the stunning photographs of those breeds that do not exist in England.
I have also sought advice from expert breeders and I offer them my grateful thanks to them for reading and checking what I have written and, where needed, supplying me with the right cats to photograph:-
TERESA COLE (Birmans), SALLY FRANKLIN (Orientals),
MARJORIE HORNETT (Bengal and Ocicat), SUE KEMPSTER (British),
SAL MARSH (Burmese) and BARONESS MIRANDA von KIRCHBERG
(Asian/Burmilla Group)
There are others whose ears I have bent for additional information, who have supplied the right feline 'models', or both, including:-
TRICIA JENKINSON, SANDRA MOORE, BRIGID OAKLEY,
ANGELA SIVYER, LINDA TAYLOR, PAT TURNER, PAM WILDING ...
and if I have left out anybody, please accept my apologies.

PHOTO CREDITS:
All photographs by PADDY CUTTS/ANIMALS UNLIMITED, except those on the following pages, for which LARRY JOHNSON is acknowledged:
51 right, 121 above right, 121 right, 150-151, 150 inset, 160, 161, 163 above

USEFUL ADDRESSES

UNITED KINGDOM
Governing Council of the Cat Fancy (GCCF)
4-6 Penel Orlieu
Bridgewater
Somerset TA6 3PG

GCCF Cat Welfare Liaison Committee
c/o Secretary
Mrs Barbara Harrington
79 Pilgrim's Way
Kemsing
Near Sevenoaks
Kent TB15 6TD

Feline Advisory Bureau
350 Upper Richmond Road
Putney
London SW15 6TL

Journals
Cats
5 James Leigh St
Manchester M1 6EX

Cat World
10 Western Road
Shoreham-by-Sea
West Sussex BN4 5WD

UNITED STATES
American Cat Association (ACA)
8101 Katherine Drive
Panorama City
CA 91402

American Cat Fanciers' Association (ACFA)
PO Box 203
Point Lookout
MO 65726

Cat Fanciers' Association (CFA Inc)
PO Box 1005
Manasquan
NJ 087361005

Cat Fanciers' Federation (CFF)
9509 Montgomery Road
Cincinnati
OH 45242

The Independent Cat Association (TICA)
PO Box 2988
Harlingen
TX 87550

Journals
Cat Fancy
PO Box 4030
San Clemente
CA 92672

Cats
445 Merrimac Drive
Port Orange
FL 32019

Cat World
PO Box 35635
Phoenix
AZ 850969

EUROPE
Fédération Internationale Féline (FIFe)
C/o Secretary
Mme R van Haeringen
23 Doerhavelaan
Eindhoven 5644 BB
Netherlands

Journal
A Tout Chat
(service des abonnements - subscriptions)
BP 205
Versailles 78003
France

AUSTRALIA
Co-ordinating Cat Council of Australia
(CCCofA)
Box No 4317
GPO
Sydney
NSW 2001

SOUTH AFRICA
Governing Council of the Associated Cat
Clubs of South Africa
C/o Mrs M Simpson
45 Edison Drive
Meadowridge 7800

C O N T E N T S

INTRODUCTION

Throughout the cat fancies of the world, there is a huge variety of pedigree cats. Some are ancient breeds that have changed little over the years. Many of these have delightful legends surrounding their ancestry. Other, new breeds have been developed by dedicated breeders and are the result of a greater understanding of the genetics of colour inheritance.

Not all breeds exist in all countries; not all countries organize the classifications of their cats in the same way. As it is difficult to please all of the people all of the time, for the purposes of this book I have based the categories on the British registration system, as used by the Governing Council of the Cat Fancy. I have 'fitted' in breeds that do not exist in this country where I feel they would be appropriate if ever they were to be imported into the United Kingdom.

It may appear a little confusing at first to find that there is a shorthaired variety in the Persian section and cats with long fur in the Shorthair, Oriental and Siamese sections - but this is for good reason! Cats are judged mainly on their type, that is, their skeletal and muscular shape. Over the years, semi-longhaired varieties of existing shorthaired breeds have cropped up, as with the Abyssinian, whose semi-longhaired version is called the Somali, and the Siamese, whose semi-longhaired equivalent is the Balinese. Similarly, in recent years a breed of full Persian type, but with a short plush coat, has been developed; it is known as the Exotic Shorthair. These are both judged and registered under their appropriate sections and these are where they will be found in this book. If in doubt, consult the index.

The type of some breeds may differ from one side of the Atlantic to the other. This is particularly noticeable in Burmese, where the American version is much chunkier with a more rounded 'apple' head than its British counterpart. Equally, some breeds have different names; for example, the Colourpoint Persian in the United Kingdom is known as a Himalayan in the United States. I have tried to point out any transatlantic differences in the text.

I have been owned by Burmese cats for nearly 20 years and this is, therefore, the breed that I know the best. However, it has been my pleasure and privilege to have been allowed to photograph many of the top winning cats of all varieties in the United Kingdom over a period of some 17 years, either in my studio or on location in the cats' own homes. It is on my personal experiences that I have based my character analysis of the various breeds. Not everybody will agree with me, but as I have been involved with cat welfare and rescue for many years, I feel very strongly that the selection of a breed should be well considered; the characters and temperaments of some breeds are not suitable to every household environment. Each cat has its own very special needs and requirements - physical and psychological. It is sad that many beautiful pedigree cats end up in rescue centres simply because their owners were unaware of the needs of the breed that they chose. So please, if you have bought this book in order to decide which breed is best for you, do not judge by the photographs alone; find the time to read the text, as this will give you a reasonable insight into each breed's behaviour.

Finally, remember that it is not so unusual for a cat to live to be 18 years or older; this roughly equates with the length of time a child would be living at home with you. Bear this in mind when making your choice.

At the end of the day, if this book stops one cat having to be re-homed due to lack of knowledge of the particular breed, it has been a worthwhile project indeed.

PERSIANS

Persians are one of the oldest breeds of pedigree cats and certainly one of the most instantly recognized because of their long, luxuriant coats. They are, sweet-natured placid and easy-going cats – laid back is a more modern term for their outlook on life! Unlike Burmese and Siamese, for example, they are not vocally noisy cats and are generally undemanding – except in terms of their grooming requirements. For many generations Persians have been selectively bred for long, silky coats with considerable undercoat; one raspy little tongue is not enough to keep the cat's coat in pristine order without a little help from a human.

P E R S I A N S

These sweet-natured cats make delightful pets, but, sadly, the main reason that they are sometimes re-homed is simply that their owners cannot cope with the time-consuming grooming that is needed.
If you cannot afford to spare 15–20 minutes on grooming each day, please choose to buy a different breed. A badly knotted Persian will have to be subjected to a general anaesthetic at the veterinary surgery in order to 'repair' its coat. This is not a pleasant experience for the cat, and is also expensive for the owner.

HISTORY

Longhaired cats have been found in many parts of the world, usually in upland regions or areas where the weather is cooler; their long, thick coats gave them excellent protection against the elements.
The earliest longhairs originated from Ankara in Turkey and became known as Angoras. This was back in the late 1800s; a decade or so later other cats displaying long fur were discovered in Persia. The original Turkish cats had longish faces and less prolific coats than the cats seen in Persia. During Victorian times in England, the newly discovered Persians became more popular, as their fur was more profuse and their shorter faces gave them a more glamorous and unusual expression. Although the Turkish cats still exist in the Cat Fancy today, they are now known as Turkish Vans and Turkish Angoras and are classified in the Semi-Longhair section (see pages 58-81). The Angora is a longhaired Oriental (see pages 194-5).
Both Persians and Siamese cats were exhibited at the first recorded cat show, which took place at the Crystal Palace in London, England, on 17 July, 1871. The earliest colours were tabby and black, but cat fancies throughout the world now recognize Persians in a myriad of colours and patterns as a result of an increased knowledge of genetics and much hard work on the part of the breeders.

COLOURS AND PATTERNS –
HOW THEY DEVELOPED

From the original Tabbies and Blacks, as well as the Blue, it was possible to create a variety of different colours and patterns. By mating to the Tortoiseshell, and thus introducing the sex-linked red gene, it was possible to produce not only Tortie Persians, but Reds and Creams, too. White Persians were probably originally related to the White Turkish Angora and when mated to the Persians, produced a white cat of more Persian type.

The Chinchilla is basically a white cat with each strand of fur being lightly tipped at the end with black. This gives the cat a 'sparkling' look, almost as if it has stepped out of the pages of a fairy tale. When the sex-linked red gene was introduced, the Golden Persian (originally called the Golden Chinchilla) had arrived.

The Shaded Silver is more densely tipped than the Chinchilla. The Pewter, a result of mating a Chinchilla to one of the Self-Colours, is even more densely tipped. The Smoke is at the far end of the tipped spectrum; where the Chinchilla is almost white, with the slightest amount of tipping, the Smoke, at first glance, looks like a Self-Colour until it moves and the pale undercoat is revealed.

The Himalayan factor was introduced into the Persian by mating a Blue Persian with a Siamese. This produced a longhaired cat with the restricted coat pattern seen in Siamese, known as the Colourpoint in the United Kingdom and the Himalayan in the United States. They are bred in just as many colours and patterns as the Siamese. A by-product of the Colourpoint breeding programme created the Self-Lilac and Self-Chocolate Persians.

Today, Persians are bred in over 60 different colours and patterns, including Tabbies in Brown, Silver, Red, Blue, Chocolate, Lilac and a whole spectrum of Tortie Tabbies and Tortoiseshell and Tortie and Whites in just as many colours. The possibilities and combinations seem almost endless, which is probably why the Persian section at most shows today has the largest number of entries.

TYPE AND JUDGING STANDARDS

Early Persians, around the turn of the century did not display the full coat that is seen on the show bench today and their faces were much longer than is sought after now. In general, the Persian is a medium to large

cat, with a strong, broad chest. The legs should be
thick and strong. The head is large and round, with
small, neat, wide-set ears and full cheeks. The eyes are
large, round and bold. The coat should be long, thick
and fine-textured without being woolly. The eye
colour varies with the coat colour, but, in general,
should be a deep orange or copper with a few
exceptions. White Persians may have blue, orange or
odd eyes (one of each colour); Chinchillas, Shaded
Silvers and Golden Persians have green or blue-green
eyes; Colourpoints have pure blue eyes. In the United
States , Persians of extreme facial type have been
developed and are known as Peke-Faced Persians; in
the United Kingdom, some British breeders have
started to produce similarly typed cats that are
generally known as 'Ultra' Persians.

The Exotic Shorthair is one of the more recent
arrivals in the Persian section. It may seen strange to
mention a shorthaired cat in this chapter, but the
Exotic is truly a cat of Persian type and is judged to
exactly the same standard of points. The only
difference is that it does not display the long coat!
This breed is sometimes confused with the British
Shorthair (see Chapter 3).

GOOD POINTS

Sweet-natured

Generally undemanding (other than grooming needs)

Have quiet voices

Good with children and other animals

Do not mind being left alone if you have to go out to
work – but prefer a bit of feline company

BAD POINTS

Need frequent, daily grooming

More prone to fur balls than other breeds

When moulting, their fur is more noticeable on the
carpets and furnishings

Can suffer from gastric upsets, so watch their diets
carefully

The more typey 'Ultra' Persians need attention paid to
their eyes, which often 'weep'; they may also have
breathing problems

May be necessary to clip their fur around the anal
region; faeces will readily adhere to the long coat

Their long coats and the grooming preparations
needed may cause an allergic reaction in their owners

PREVIOUS PAGES: *The Self-Black Persian should have a profuse black coat which is completely solid to the roots. In kittenhood, the coat may show some shading or even faint tabby markings. These are permissible in a kitten but should fade by the time the cat has become adult, when they would be considered serious faults. In* the summer months, an over-indulgence in sunbathing may result in a slightly copper hue! Both these cats were allowed outside access – but only in a completely fenced in 'cat-proof' garden. Any cat allowed to wander freely should always be supplied with a properly designed, safe cat collar and an identity disc.

BELOW AND OPPOSITE: *The Self-Blue is one of the older colours of Persians and is rumoured to have been Queen Victoria's favourite breed of cat. It is still one of the best-known and best-loved of this breed. Both these cats show that their coats have been regularly maintained and are groomed to a level of perfection.*

PREVIOUS PAGES: *Self-Chocolate is one of the by-products of the Colourpoint breeding programme and one of the newer self-colours. The coat should be an even mid-chocolate colour that is sound to the roots and without any shading or white hairs.*

PREVIOUS PAGES, INSET: *Lustrous, deep copper-coloured eyes stand out to superb effect against the solid, glossy, jet black coat. This cat has very good ear set too, just as the standards require: small neat ears set low and well apart on the head.*

BELOW: *Cream is another well-established colour that still retains much popularity. This pale cream coat is not the easiest to keep in sparkling condition and many of the paler coloured Persians will benefit from a regular bath to keep their coats clean, even if they are not destined for the show bench.*

ABOVE: *This young Cream displays the type referred to in the United Kingdom as 'Ultra', which is similar to the Peke-Faced in the United States. The face is much flatter and the nose shorter than those of the more conventional Persian type.*

FOLLOWING PAGES: *The Self-Lilac, like the Chocolate, is a result of the Colourpoint breeding programme. As with the Colourpoints, these cats are distantly related to the Siamese and so tend to have rather more outgoing personalities than some of the traditional Persian colours. Both Chocolate and Lilac are useful outcrosses for Colourpoint breeding.*

BELOW: *Red is a difficult colour to breed with a completely clear coat, as is required for the Self-Colours in general. The standards allow for Reds to show slight shading on the head and legs but nowhere else. However, the rich red coat and the deep copper eyes make for a most attractive colour combination.*

RIGHT AND BELOW: *Blue-eyed Whites have frequently been associated with deafness. This may be a risk when this colour combination is seen in a non-pedigree cat, but hearing problems are not common in the pedigree varieties. It is often thought that entire male cats can be aggressive towards kittens, but this fine gentleman (right) seems to be very proud of his little Pewter son.*

PREVIOUS PAGES: *This orange-eyed White is a real credit to his owner. His immaculate appearance has not been achieved by a quick bath and brush-up the day before the photograph was taken, but is the result of regular grooming started when he was a small kitten and continued every day of his luxurious life.*

PREVIOUS PAGES, INSET: *Whites may have three distinct eye colourings and these siblings are odd-eyed (left) and orange-eyed (right). Although all kittens are born with blue eyes, the eye colour will start to change at about eight weeks. Even in kittens as young as these two, it is quite clear that one has the odd-eyed colour.*

BELOW AND OPPOSITE: *As the cat matures, the difference in the eye colour will become even more apparent as these two cats demonstrate. Although these cats are the same breed, the one below was bred some 10 years earlier than the one opposite. As with most things, it is a matter of personal preference; some breeders prefer the older type and others the shorter face of the latter.*

LEFT AND BELOW: *Bi-Colours are a mixture of any of the solid or tabby colours and white. It is important that the white makes up no less than one-third and no more than half of the whole coat; the face should have both colours. The Blue Bi-Colour (left) shows the most striking, white markings on his face while the Cream (below) displays a lovely, even colour distribution. Both conform beautifully to the standards.*

RIGHT AND BELOW: *The standards for Blue Creams are quite different on one side of the Atlantic from the other. These two Blue Creams conform perfectly to the Governing Council of the Cat Fancy standards, which require an evenly mingled mixture of blue and cream without any solid patches of colour. In the United States, it is quite the opposite. There, they prefer clearly defined patches of the two colours. In both countries, it is considered a fault for any patches of white to be present.*

ABOVE AND OPPOSITE: *Cameos are another of the tipped varieties with varying densities of shading. They have a white undercoat with light red or cream tipping in the Shell and a denser amount of colour in the Shaded. They are also seen in Tortie and Blue Cream colours. The cat in the photograph above is a Cream Shaded, the one on the top of the page opposite is a Tortie and that opposite below is a Red Shaded.*

PREVIOUS PAGES: *Chinchillas are slightly different from the mainstream Persians; they may be slightly lighter boned and are generally more elegant. Apart from the magnificent tipped coat, the Chinchilla has the most striking facial markings. The green eyes are outlined in black, making the cat look as if it is wearing mascara. The brick red nose leather is also outlined in black, giving the cat a most distinctive appearance.*

BELOW: *Colourpoints, although definitely of Persian type, display the restricted Himalayan coat patterning of the Siamese. They are a 'man-made' breed, one of the most popular among Persians. This is a fine example of a Blue Point.*

BELOW AND RIGHT: *The Seal Point (below) was one of the earliest colours to be developed and today there are as many different colours as there are in Siamese. The Tortie Point (right) gave rise to the Reds and Creams.*

OPPOSITE: *This superb Cream Point gained the ultimate accolade when he became overall Best Exhibit at the Governing Council of the Cat Fancy Supreme Show. He is probably as near to perfection as one could find. His pale coat, with the colour restricted to just the face, ears, legs and tail, has been beautifully groomed. The eye colour and set are just as they should be. The face is exactly right, with the typical Persian expression. No wonder he won this high award!*

RIGHT: *The Tortie Tabby (Torbie in the United States) is a mixture of tabby overlaid with tortie markings.*

BELOW AND OPPOSITE: *The Golden Persians came by way of the Chinchilla, some of which carry the red gene. They were first called Golden Chinchillas, with the darker marked ones being known as Shaded Goldens. This roughly equates with the relationship between the Chinchilla and the Shaded Silver. The photographs show a Golden Persian (below) and a Golden and Shaded Golden (opposite).*

OPPOSITE, RIGHT AND BELOW:
Pewter and Shaded Silvers are also related to the Chinchilla. The Pewter (opposite), is much more darkly tipped than the Chinchilla, but not so deeply as the Smoke. The Shaded (right and below), is slightly darker tipped than the Chinchilla and is sometimes thought of as an inferior Chinchilla. Some fancies recognize the Shaded as a separate breed, but not all of them.

Cats

PREVIOUS PAGES: *Tabbies have long been extremely popular, perhaps because their 'wild cat' coat pattern reminds us of the origins of the domestic cat. The Brown Tabby is the oldest of the tabby colours.*

BELOW: *Smokes are bred in a variety of colours. The coat is almost the reverse of the Chinchilla: the colour extends almost the entire length of each hair shaft and it is only the very base level of the coat that is pale coloured.*

OPPOSITE: *Tabby and White is another of the newer patterns and, in the United Kingdom, this variety has yet to be granted Championship status. They are accepted in as many colours as the other tabbies, and it is important that the white parts should be completely free of any shading of any other colour.*

FOLLOWING PAGES: *Persian kittens do look like little bundles of fluff and are so cute and immediately appealing. Please remember, however, that they do not stay kittens for very long and the fully adult coat will take much patient and time-consuming grooming.*

46

OPPOSITE: *The coat colour of the Blue Tabby and White is blue on a beige agouti background; the white areas should have no marks or tones of other colours.*

RIGHT AND BELOW: *The Red Tabby Peke-Faced Persian (right) is an American breed of extreme type: a very short, flat face and a small, short nose. In Britain this roughly equates with what is termed the 'Ultra' Persian. The British-bred Red Tabby Persian (below) shows quite different type and is not so short in the face. Both display the rich red coat with even deeper red markings that are so sought after in this colour.*

Cats

PREVIOUS PAGES: *Silver cats of all breeds are extremely popular at present. This Silver Tabby shows why. The jet black markings set off against a silver background are a striking combination.*

FOLLOWING PAGES: *The Blue Tortie and White has the same standards as the Tortie and White. Only the colour is different. It should be a mixture of a medium pale blue and cream.*

FOLLOWING PAGES, INSET: *This Blue Exotic Shorthair may seem out of place in the Persian section. It is a cat of true Persian type that has been selectively bred to produce Persian type and temperament, but with a short, plush coat. This breed would be a good choice for someone who would love to own a Persian, but could not put up with all the grooming or is, perhaps, allergic to the long fur! Exotics are accepted in all the colours recognized for Persians, and in seven colours of Spotted Tabby.*

OPPOSITE: *Although Torties are bred in a wide range of colours today, it is the Black Tortoiseshell that is considered the classic and traditional tortie colour, as it was the original. The coat should be a good mixture of black broken with red, evenly distributed throughout the coat.*

BELOW: *The Tortie and White is a mixture of black and red patches splendidly set off against a white background. The white parts should not take up more than half and no less than one-third of the coat.*

54

SEMI-LONGHAIRS

The Semi-Longhair section contains cats which display long fur, but are not of Persian type, and do not have a shorthair equivalent. It includes some very old breeds, such as the Birman and Turkish Van, but also quite a few newcomers! Although they have completely different origins, histories, temperaments and needs, there are a few character traits that they share. In general, although the fur of these breeds requires more grooming than that of shorthaired cats, it does not need so much attention as that of a Persian. Their coats, while long and silky, tend to be less thick and so are less prone to knotting and matting.

SEMI-LONGHAIRS

The personalities of this group are more outgoing than Persians', but they are not usually so demanding as some of the shorthair breeds, such as Burmese and Siamese. They generally have sweet, placid natures, are not spiteful and make excellent family pets.

(For Angora, see Orientals and for Balinese, see Siamese.)

Birman

This is a most distinctive breed, originating from Burma. It has a long, silky coat that is pale in colour with darker points on the face, legs and tail. Unlike other breeds showing the restricted Himalayan factor, the Birman's toes are white. The face is slightly pointed, but not so long as the Balinese. The Birman is sometimes confused with other breeds: Burmese (from the similarity of the names and the country of origin), Balinese (the semi-longhaired Siamese) and the Colourpoint (a breed of Persian type with the restricted coat pattern of the Siamese).

A delightful legend tells how the Birman acquired its white paws and deep blue eyes. The temple of Lao-Tsun was the home of a beautiful blue-eyed golden goddess, who presided over the souls of priests. The holiest priests were allowed to live on after death in the body of a holy animal for as long as the animal lived. The high priest's favourite temple cat was pale coloured with dark ears, nose, tail and legs. As the elderly priest lay dying, the cat came to visit him and gently rested his paws on the old man's chest to offer companionship, devotedly staying beside him until he died. So good was the priest that his soul went straight to heaven and the eyes of his devoted cat turned a brilliant blue and its paws turned the purest white as a symbol of loyalty. It is said that every time a Birman cat dies, the soul of a priest accompanies it to heaven.

Birmans are intelligent, playful and love to be part of a family – both human and feline. They are inquisitive, exploring and adventurous, but seem to have more sense than some of the Foreign Shorthairs; Birmans do not normally get themselves into situations where they have to be rescued. The original Birman was Seal Brown but, as with most breeds, they are seen today in a variety of colours, including Blue, Chocolate, Red, Cream, Tortie and Tabby Points. Whatever the colour of the points, it is most important that they have symmetrical 'gloves' (the markings on the forelegs), which should not extend further than the tops of the paws and end in a straight line, and gauntlets (markings on the back legs), which cover the whole paw and stretch up to the back of the hock in a 'V' shape. Birmans are of medium size, with a broad, rounded head tapering to a strong chin; in profile, the nose should show a slight dip. The eyes are blue and rounded.

MAINE COON

This has long been a popular breed in the United States, but it has only recently become established in the United Kingdom. As the name suggests, these cats were first noted in the state of Maine. The 'coon' part of the name refers to the brushlike tail similar to a raccoon's. Legend says that the Maine Coon first arrived in America when Marie Antoinette sent her beloved cats there to escape the perils of the French Revolution. How true this is is anyone's guess, but they do bear a striking resemblance to native European cats.

One of the Maine Coon's most striking features is its thick, dense, heavy and waterproof coat, which protects it against the fiercely cruel New England winters. It needs little extra grooming and is virtually self-maintaining – a definite plus for anyone wanting for a longhaired breed but with little time for constant grooming! It is a strong, heavily-built and rugged breed. The adult is a very large cat, indeed – be warned, this is not the breed for you if you prefer a dainty, elegant feline! The standards call for a medium-long head, with a square muzzle and firm chin. The ears are large and tall, set high on the head, but well apart and tapering to a point at the tip. The muscular body should appear rectangular with a square rump. The tail is long – at least the length of the cat's back. Maine Coons are characterful cats, interesting and intelligent; while they love to play games with their owners, they are also extremely adept at playing their own games. Their excellence at catching mice is not, however, an adequate reason for keeping one of these beautiful creatures; all cats are pets and should be treated as such.

NORWEGIAN FOREST CAT

In many ways, the Norwegian Forest Cat looks very similar to the Maine Coon. It is another big, strong breed with a dense, waterproof coat, but it has a daintier, more refined face and a huge, plume-like tail.

They are said to be excellent climbers, capable of scaling an almost sheer mountain face. Norse legends tell of a mountain-dwelling 'fairy cat' with a sweet expression that was able to climb higher than any other cat known. Perhaps this is the modern version.

The standards call for a triangular head, with a long, straight profile and large, slightly slanted eyes. The ears are tufted, rather like a lynx. The bushy tail should reach at least as far as the neck, when held against the body, and the fur should be particularly long in these two areas. Norwegians are accepted in almost all colours and patterns.

Norwegians are reputed to be excellent hunters and will benefit from and enjoy the freedom of a garden. Their sweet natures make them excellent pets, but they do love human company and do not like being left alone.

RAGDOLL

This is a breed with a restricted coat pattern, not dissimilar to Colourpoints, Birmans and the short-coated Siamese. A relatively new breed, it gained recognition in the United States in the 1960s but it is only since the 1970s that it has been seen in the United Kingdom, where it was granted preliminary status with the Governing Council of the Cat Fancy in 1992.

This breed is somewhat controversial. Ragdolls will 'flop' in your arms when they are held and this, supposedly, makes them different from other breeds. They emanate from California, where a White Persian, who had mis-mated, suffered a broken pelvis in a car accident and 'flopped' in the arms of her owner. When the kittens were born, they displayed the same 'floppiness'. Perhaps they were damaged *in utero*.

Nevertheless, an accident cannot cause a genetic mutation and any cat will 'flop' in your arms if it feels secure and loved. Ragdolls are also reputed to feel no pain and reports in the popular press emphasize that they enjoy being tossed and thrown. Never believe the tabloids! Ragdolls are cats, whatever their origin, and should never be treated as a child's plaything, from which their name seems to have been derived!

The fancies require the Ragdoll to be medium-sized with a muscular body. It has a medium length head, a wide, flat forehead, and medium-sized, low-set ears. In profile, the nose should show a shallow, gentle break and a firm chin. The eyes are large, oval and deep blue in colour. The coat patterns allowed are Colourpointed, Mitted and Bi-Colour; within each of these patterns Seal, Blue, Chocolate and Lilac are accepted.

Despite their curious history, Ragdolls are a delightful breed with a sweet nature. They are relatively undemanding and relaxed in most situations.

(For Somali, see Other Shorthairs, Abyssinian and for Tiffanie, see Other Shorthairs, Burmilla/Asian group.)

TURKISH VAN

The Turkish Van is an old breed that originated from the Lake Van district of upland eastern Turkey. Unlike most cats, who generally do not like water, it is a swimming cat. Turkish like to live somewhere with access to a small, shallow (for safety) pool; if not, they'll probably want to join you in the bath! They have outgoing personalities and enjoy both feline and human company.

The first longhairs seen in England were Angoras, which came from another part of Turkey, and it was not until the 1950s that Vans were brought to Britain and a breeding programme was started. There are similarities between Vans and Angoras, but the original Angoras were white, whereas the Turkish Van has distinctive auburn markings set off against a white coat. The two breeds are sometimes confused, but they are quite different. Auburn markings confined to the head and tail are commonly seen in the shorthaired street cats of Istanbul, rather in the way that tabby seems to be the predominant pattern of the indigenous European cat. They were originally seen to have a distinct white or cream 'thumb-print' marking between the ears of an otherwise auburn mask – said to be the mark of Allah. Nowadays, this is now considered a fault if it is irregularly placed.

The standard of points today requires the Turkish Van to be a long, sturdy, well-muscled cat. The head should show a long nose, with a short wedge, but with a minimal dip in the profile. The fur is long and soft and should be more prominent on the tail, head and ears. Turkish are interesting cats, with outgoing personalities. They need little grooming other than the regular care needed for any Semi-Longhair. If you can cope with their need for water – they make excellent pets.

OPPOSITE AND BELOW: *Birmans are an old breed and legends tell that they were the sacred cats of the Burmese temples. Two of the most popular colours are Seal Point (opposite) and Blue Point (below).*

PREVIOUS PAGES: *Birmans are a very elegant and distinctive breed and should always show well-matched white socks and gauntlets.*

BELOW: *The Maine Coon is native to the North American state of Maine. It has a thick, dense, waterproof coat to protect it from harsh winter weather conditions in New England.*

OPPOSITE AND FOLLOWING PAGES: *Maine Coons are bred in a multitude of colours and patterns. Some people think of the 'classic' Maine Coon as a Tabby and White (opposite) or Tabby (following pages).*

BELOW AND OPPOSITE: *The Norwegian Forest cat has a thick, waterproof coat similar to the Maine Coon and may well have been a descendant of the 'fairy cat' referred to in Norse legend.*

BELOW AND OPPOSITE: *Ragdolls are bred in three basic patterns: Bi-Colour (bottom), Mitted (below) and Colourpointed (opposite).*

PREVIOUS PAGES, OPPOSITE AND ABOVE: *Breeding programmes in the United Kingdom have made way for newer colours of Birman. The Tortie Point (previous page) originated by mating a Seal Point Birman to a long-faced Cream Persian. Tabby Birmans (opposite) stem from one of two* sources; *some lines are descended from an original mis-mate with a non-pedigree cat, while others emanate from a mating between a Birman and a Tabby Colourpoint Persian. The Cream Point (above) is the result of the introduction of the red sex-linked gene from the Tortie.* FOLLOWING PAGES: *Although Turkish Vans have recently been bred with both blue and odd eyes, and have also been produced in the dilute Cream form, it is still the original – and classic – Auburn Turkish with amber eyes that is the best-known and best-loved of this breed.*

British, European and American Shorthairs

The British, European and American Shorthairs could well be described as the 'gentle giants' of the cat world: big, beautiful felines with sweet, gentle dispositions that belie their size. As kittens, they look rather like little cuddly teddy bears, but please be warned! That dear little kitten is going to grow into a very large cat, so be sure that you like the adult version as much as the kitten.

British, European and American Shorthairs

Kittens are little for only a few months; the adult cat will be with you for many years to come. Be absolutely certain that you want a big cat and do not, a year later, allow one of these delightful, friendly animals to become yet another rescue statistic.

History

Their history goes back centuries; shorthaired cats with heavy bone structure were recorded as far back as ancient Roman times. These cats were quite different from the ancient Egyptian cats that resembled the breed we now call the Abyssinian. It seems quite likely that these solid, shorthaired cats were first taken to England with the invading Roman troops, who would have found them useful for keeping mice away from their food stores.

As short hair is genetically dominant to long hair and shorthaired cats are more self-sufficient in the wild than their longhaired counterparts, it is possible that the American Shorthairs developed independently of the British. It is equally possible that they first arrived in America with the Pilgrim Fathers. This is only speculation. Although cats of British type have been depicted in many works of art over the years, it is only since the beginning of this century that there have been written records of the British breed as it is known today.

Colours and patterns –
how they developed

The earliest recorded British cats were Tabbies. These are still popular on the show bench today, especially the glamorous Silver Tabbies, but it is the Self-Colour cats that are the best-known and also the favourites. Black and Blue are two of the older varieties which still retain popularity. Tortoiseshell females, which carry the sex-linked red gene, gave rise to the Red and Cream colours, both of which are extremely difficult to breed for clear coat colour. British Bi-Colours are a mixture of white and any of the recognized solid colours; Tortie and White cats, which are known as Calico in the United States, are an equal mixture of white and tortie.

As cat fanciers began to understand more about genetics, a myriad of other colour possibilities arose. If a Colourpoint Persian could be produced by crossing a Persian with a Siamese, would it not be possible to introduce the Himalayan factor into the British breed, too? As the Persian type resembles the British more closely than the Siamese, and the Colourpoint Longhair was already in existence, it seemed obvious to mate the two. This breeding programme gave rise to the Chocolate/Lilac series, which can be colourpointed carriers.

TYPE AND JUDGING STANDARDS

To generalize, the British cat is solid, muscular, chunky and heavily boned. They grow to be large cats, the males being considerably bigger than the females and male neuters often larger still.

The head is large and broad with small, neat ears set wide apart on the head. The males should show typical masculine 'jowls'. The eyes are large and round and, with the exception of Manx, Tabbies, Colourpointed and Whites, their colour can vary from gold to orange or copper. The nose is short and, in profile, should show a definite 'stop'. A deep, broad chest is preferred and the legs should be short and sturdy with neat, rounded paws. The tail is short and thickset; it should never be thin or whiplike, as required for the Siamese, for example.

There are a number of subtle differences between the standards required for the British, European and American fancies.

British cats in the United Kingdom conform to the general standard, except in some of the Tabby series, which tend to be less bulky and lighter boned and do not grow to be so massive as the other colours of British Shorthairs.

In Europe, the standards are exactly the same as those required by the Governing Council of the Cat Fancy, with the exception of the Chartreux. This is similar to the British Blue and, in some fancies, it is judged to the same standard. Purists maintain that it is a unique, old breed, originally kept by the monks of the order of La Grande Chartreuse in France, and that it is distinct from the British Blue. Where it classified as a separate breed, the cat is generally less massive than its British counterpart, the head is slightly more elongated, the ears a little larger and the coat should show distinct silver ticking. The eye colour should be a definite gold, rather than the British copper colour.

The American Shorthair is more muscled than the British, with slightly lighter bone structure and a longer face. In all other respects, the American Shorthairs should correspond to the general standard for British and are bred in just as many coat colours and patterns, the commonest being the Tabby series.

The Manx, although generally categorized as 'British', is a breed set completely apart. The only reason that these cats appear in this section is because geographically, they emanate from the Isle of Man, one of the British Isles! Quite how this tailless variety of cat was caused is debatable. Any island remote from a mainland country or with little trading access has to have a limited 'gene-pool'. Any animal displaying a recessive gene in its phenotype will, inevitably, pass this on to its progeny. Not all will display the tailless factor and this explains the 'tailed' Manx syndrome. Almost all Manx cats will produce a mixture of rumpies (completely tailless), stumpies and rumpy risers (Manx with a tiny vestigial tail) and fully tailed kittens. The texture of their fur is different from the other British Shorthairs, being a thicker 'double' coat which requires more grooming. They are acceptable in almost any colour and pattern. The Manx have longer back legs than most breeds, giving rise to their distinctive 'rabbity' gait.

GOOD POINTS

Friendly, gentle cats with sweet natures

Do not grumble and groan if left for a few hours on
their own

Generally, are not destructive

Good with young children, as they are not spiteful

Equally good with older people, as they are not as
active as the foreign breeds

A typical fireside cat – 'the next best thing to a
moggie' or non-pedigree cat, as one British breeder
puts it!

BAD POINTS

They are large when adult and need more food than
most breeds until they reach maturity

Their thick coats require weekly grooming – a little
more than other shorthairs

Manx need regular, daily grooming, as their thick
coats are prone to forming mats

ABOVE: *Although it is preferred for British Black kittens to have a solid black coat, it is acceptable in a kitten for the coat to show a slight 'rusty' hue, as this delightful little girl shows. In an adult this would be considered a bad fault and quite unacceptable. It is not always possible to assess the quality of a kitten when it is only ten weeks old, and this one is just beginning to show the change in eye colour. The breeder had great faith in the kitten's potential and was certainly proved correct. Look at the photograph opposite; this is the same cat as a young adult after she had gained not only the title of Champion, but Grand Champion, too.*

OPPOSITE: *Black is one of the oldest-known colours of any breed of cat, not just the British. Over the years, black cats have had their fair share of ups and downs; at worst, they were considered agents of the devil and witches' familiars and were burned at stake and, at best, when the popularity stakes were at their highest, a symbol of good luck! The British Black conforms in general to the standards laid down for Self-Colour British but tends to have a sleeker, glossier coat than the other colours. The deep copper-gold eyes, strikingly set off by a jet black coat, makes for one of the most attractive of all the British Shorthairs.*

PREVIOUS PAGES: *The Blue is probably the best known and most popular of all the British colours. The short, dense coat is easy to groom, but for show perfection, the solid colours will benefit from a few days in a cool, or better still, an outdoor environment so that the coat becomes 'crisp'. British should not have a coat that feels soft to the touch. This cat shows the correct medium blue coat colour, which should be solid to the roots without any silver ticking, and the required compact, powerful body so typical of this breed.*

PREVIOUS PAGES, INSET: *As with all kittens, the British Blue goes through a phase where the coat is a little 'fluffy'. There may even be a few vestigial 'ghost' tabby markings, such as stripes, rings or bars. These are quite acceptable in a kitten, as they will usually even out as the cat matures, but if present in an adult cat, would preclude the certificate being awarded.*

BELOW: *The British Chocolate is a relative newcomer to the Self-Colours. As with the Lilac (see page 96), it is a 'by-product' of the British Colourpointed breeding programme. Although it has only preliminary status with the Governing Council of the Cat Fancy, the rich, brown coat is most attractive and Chocolates are becoming popular.*

OPPOSITE: *One of the most appealing features of the British Blue is its large, round, lustrous copper or deep golden coloured eyes. These, together with the round, full-cheeked face and neat ears, give the British the sweetest expression, perfectly reflecting this breed's kind and gentle disposition.*

PREVIOUS PAGES: *Over the years, the coat of the Cream has become much clearer. The early Creams, such as this, were the results of mating British Shorthairs with Persians. This gave the Creams of the time much shorter faces – almost 'exotic' in type – and many showed quite obvious tabby markings. As a result of selective breeding programmes, these faults have been almost eliminated in the Creams of the 1990s.*

PREVIOUS PAGES, INSET: *The British Cream is another of the Self-Colours and the coat should be an even, pale cream. It is very difficult to breed this colour completely 'bar-free' – and the*

standards require that the coat is as free from markings as possible. This handsome animal shows only the faintest 'rings' on his tail and a few tabby markings on his paws.

BELOW: *As with the Chocolate, the Lilac British occurred as a result of the Colourpointed breeding programme. Both the Chocolate and Lilac are Self-Colours and have the typical British deep gold or copper eyes. The Colourpointed series has blue eyes, as do all cats with the restricted Himalayan coat pattern. This photograph shows a father and daughter study; dad is a typical male, with large jowls, while his daughter,*

although still a kitten, shows the more delicate, feminine look.

OPPOSITE: *British Whites are bred with three different eye colours: orange-eyed, blue-eyed and odd-eyed. This is an example of an odd-eyed White. These phenotypically white cats are genotypically masking other colours and the root colour will often be apparent in very young kittens. A blue-based White will show faint blue markings on the head, a black-based, black markings and so on. This gives the owner or breeder a useful insight into the genetic make-up of the cat. These markings will clear by the time the cat becomes an adult.*

PREVIOUS PAGES: *To keep these cats in pristine condition, it will be necessary for them to be bathed. Water and cats – with the very occasional exception – do not get on with each other, so it is sensible to get a kitten used to regular bathing sessions at an early age, especially if it is destined for a career on the show bench. Particular attention should be paid to the area around the eyes, as this is liable to become 'tear-stained'.*

BELOW: *British Bi-Colours are a combination of white and any of the recognized self-colours. The self-coloured base markings should be as symmetrically distributed as possible on the white coat. This Cream and White cat shows a white facial blaze, with a minimum of cream in it; for perfection, Bi-Colours should have no colour in the blaze.*

OPPOSITE: *Perfect symmetrical markings are the ideal, but they are not always seen. This Blue and White Bi-Colour kitten shows near perfect markings, even down to the blue patches on her belly. With any Self-Colour, the nose leather and paw pads should reflect the colour of the coat; with Bi-Colours, this may be either pink, in harmony with the white, or reflect the base coat colour. It is preferred that white should make up at least one-third, but no more than half of the coat.*

BELOW: *Blue Cream, although classified separately from the other Tortie colours, is still a Tortie variety. Tortoiseshell is a sex-linked pattern and torties are almost invariably female, with only the occasional, usually infertile, male being seen in this pattern. The blue and cream should be evenly mingled, without any obviously solid patches of either colour and with all four paws 'broken' with cream. The nose leather and paw pads can be blue, pink or a mixture of the two. This particular cat is an early example and has more nose break than is considered desirable today.*

OPPOSITE: *It is only comparatively recently that the Colourpointed British have become popular, although they have been bred by the dedicated few for many years. It was not until the 1970s that a structured breeding programme was implemented and, today, the Colourpointed series is found in all recognized colours, including Self, Tortie, Tabby and Tortie-Tabby Pointed. This is an example of a Blue Pointed. Whatever the colour of the points, there should always be a good contrast between them and the body colour. Shading is permissible, but it should complement the colour of the points.*

PREVIOUS PAGES: *Although this Chocolate Colourpointed British is an example of one of the newer colours, she shows perfection in her coat markings. There is a clear distinction between the pale coat and the darker points and she has the typical bold, round eyes of the British in general, with excellent blue eye colour.*

PREVIOUS PAGES, INSET: *This photograph clearly demonstrates that, whatever the coat colour or pattern, the type of British cats is essentially the same – a chunky, solid cat with a large, round head and full, apple cheeks. These two are both females, although the Colourpointed (left) is a kitten and still has much maturing to do before she is at her peak. In general, the Colourpointed varieties tend to have extremely good temperaments; the Torties (right), of this and any other breed, are rather wilful and are not known as 'naughty torties' without good reason!*

RIGHT: *This Blue Colourpointed British (left) and his Blue Cream Pointed sister (right) show noticeable differences in their markings. As in a Blue Cream British, the colour is well-mingled on the points and the Blue Pointed shows an excellent coat contrast. As with any breed showing the Himalayan factor, the coat colour in kittens is much paler than that seen in the adult cat; as the kittens mature, their coat colour changes, becoming darker and more shaded.*

OPPOSITE: *As with all Smokes, Smoke British are recognized in just as many colours as the Self-Colours and Tortie patterns. The Black Smoke is probably one of the best known, but the untrained eye can easily confuse it with a Self Black. The main difference is that Smokes are not solid to the roots and show a paler, silver undercoat. The top two-thirds of each strand of fur is black and the lower portion is silver. This becomes apparent when the coat is moved. Sometimes the eyes of Smokes may tend to have a greenish rim, especially if they have been bred from a Silver Tabby, but the desirable and correct eye colour is deep gold or copper.*

FOLLOWING PAGES: *Tabbies can be seen in different patterns and colourways. This is an example of a Red Spotted Tabby at eight months old. He may seem big for his age, but British Shorthairs do grow quickly and the males become very large cats! As with all Spotted Tabbies, the spots should be broken along the spine without any trace of a solid line of colour. The spots should be evenly patterned all over the cat, even on the belly. The paws and tail should show distinct tabby rings.*

FOLLOWING PAGES, INSET: *Typical of the British, the large, round eyes show a deep gold or copper hue. The Tabbies should show a characteristic 'M' marking on their foreheads and this can be seen clearly here. This cat still shows a 'kittenish' expression and has not developed the typical jowls of an adult male as he was neutered before maturity. The spots are quite clear along his back and the tail shows the required rings. As a rule, the Tabbies are not usually so massive as the Self-Colours.*

BELOW AND OPPOSITE: *Along with the Colourpointed and Tipped British Shorthairs, the Silver Tabbies are the only other colours that do not have the typical copper-gold eyes; the correct colour for these Silvers is green. For this reason, mating between Silver Tabbies and the Self-Colours should be done with caution, unless part of a Blue or Brown Tabby breeding programme, as the eye colour will suffer. Silver Spotted Tabbies are possibly one of the most glamorous of the British patterns, but there are also Blue, Brown and Red. Recent developments include Blue Silver, Red Silver, etc., and these can currently be seen in the assessment classes at the* Governing Council of the Cat Fancy *shows. All Tabbies should have corresponding base colours and the tabby markings should be sound to the roots; Silver Tabbies have a silver base, Blue Tabbies a biscuit-coloured base and so on.*

BELOW: *The classic tabby, whatever the breed and parentage, has always been a favourite cat. The Silver Tabby British is no exception and is a most appealing cat. When viewed from above, the shoulders should show typical butterfly markings, an unbroken black line should run the length of the spine with a stripe on either side and the neck should show a series of unbroken 'necklaces'. Each flank should show an oyster-shaped patch surrounded – for perfection – with one or more rings.*

OPPOSITE: *Although this cat is still a kitten, the correct rings on the tail can be seen, along with the oysters on the flanks. The head clearly shows the required 'M' marking, albeit a little pale. The markings will increase in density as the cat gets older.*

RIGHT: *This photograph shows a classic tabby pattern with the correct spotted belly markings, barred legs and complete tail rings. The markings should always be as symmetrical as possible, which this kitten demonstrates rather well.*

FOLLOWING PAGES: *The British Shorthaired Tipped is essentially a shorthaired Chinchilla and shows some typically Chinchilla markings. The nose leather should be brick red outlined in black and the eyes are also outlined in black so that the cat looks as if it is wearing mascara or eyeliner. The short, plush coat is a pale silver, almost white in colour, evenly tipped at the extremes with black. This gives it an almost 'sparkling' appearance and, as the cat moves, the undercoat can be seen. Although the Silver Tipped is the best-known, British Tipped are now bred in all the self and tortie colours but in some of these colours the definition of the tipping is not so pronounced as in the Silver.*

Cats

BELOW: *Tortoiseshell cats are almost always a female only variety and the best-known is the Black Tortie. This, in the British, is a well-mingled mixture of black, red and cream. The feet should always be 'broken' with red or cream and the eye colour is deep gold or copper. Newer colours of Tortie include dilutes, such as Chocolate Tortie, Lilac Tortie and Tortie and White (Calico in the United States), which should have quite distinct patches of single colours set off against a white background.*

ABOVE: *No two torties are the same; this is what gives them such appeal. Both this cat and the one shown on the previous page are perfectly good examples of British Tortoiseshells.*

ABOVE RIGHT AND RIGHT: *American Shorthairs are longer and rangier than the British. They do not display the same cobby bodies and their heads tend to be longer and narrower. The Silver Tabby (above right) is quite different in type from the British Silver Tabbies featured earlier. The differences can be clearly seen if you compare the Black and White Bi-Colour (right) and the Bi-Colour British (page 100). The GCCF standards require Bi-Colours to be evenly marked, but this is not a prerequisite under the rules of American fancies.*

PREVIOUS PAGES: *Stumpies or rumpy risers are a most useful addition to the Manx breeding programme. Although these cats cannot be shown in the United Kingdom, they still have the typical Manx temperament and make wonderful pets.*

ABOVE

RIGHT: *The Cymric is basically a longhaired Manx. Although they have been recorded in litters born to Manx cats in Britain, a breeding programme has not been pursued. The reverse is the case in the United States, where the Cymric is a most popular variety.*

RIGHT: *The Manx is one of the oldest natural breeds of cat. Although Manx have been through phases where they were not the most fashionable of felines, they are now becoming increasingly popular. The classic Manx is the rumpy, the completely tailless variety, and this is the only Manx that can be shown under the Governing Council of the Cat Fancy rules. A large part of the charm of Manx has nothing to do with their taillessness; it is their sweet natures, intelligence, dog-like devotion and longevity that endear them to cat lovers.*

OPPOSITE: *The tailed Manx seems an anomaly – surely Manx are tailless cats? Not always so and it is not uncommon for a tailed kitten to be born in a Manx litter. These cats, like all Manx, have much longer back legs than front legs, which gives rise to the Manx's typical 'rabbity' gait. The tailed Manx is becoming increasingly popular in the United States, where it may be shown under the Any Other Variety Shorthair section.*

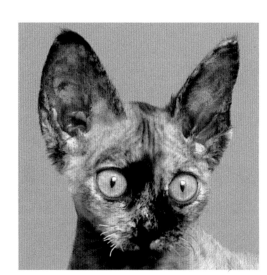

In Britain, the Governing Council of the Cat Fancy has a 'Foreigns' category. For the purposes of this book, this section includes all of this category plus those shorthaired breeds recognized in the United States and Europe but not in Britain. It also includes any of the Semi-Longhair cats with a shorthaired equivalent. It is a complex section, as all the breeds are completely different, in type, origin, temperament and needs. This group is lively and intelligent. They are not so demonstrative as the Burmese, Siamese and Orientals, but have more outgoing personalities than the British Shorthairs and the Persians.

OTHER SHORTHAIRS

Abyssinian
This shorthair breed was first seen in the United Kingdom in the mid-1800s. The original cats were probably imported from Abyssinia, now Ethiopia. Although the Semi-Longhair version, known as the Somali, had occasionally cropped up in Abyssinian litters in the United Kingdom, it was not until the late 1970s that a pair of Somalis was taken to the United Kingdom from the United States and even more recently, in 1991, that the Usual and Sorrel were granted Championship status.

American Wirehair and American Curl
These are both newer American breeds, not yet seen in Britain. The Wirehair has a wavy, wiry coat with a springy texture. It is a medium-sized, well-muscled cat, with a rounded, medium-sized head and large, round eyes. It is accepted in most colours. Both the shorthaired and longhaired American Curl have distinctive large, round-tipped ears that, uniquely, curl away from the face. It is a medium-sized, well-built cat that is accepted in any colour or pattern.

Asian Burmilla Group
The original Burmilla litter came from an accidental mating between a Lilac Burmese female and a Chinchilla male in 1981. The silver shorthair kittens, similar to Burmese in type had the 'tipped' coat of the Chinchilla. They caused such interest that their owner, Baroness Miranda von Kirchberg, considered perpetuating them as a breed and sought advice from geneticists and permission from the Burmese Cat Club to implement a breeding programme. Within this group, the term Burmilla now applies only to shaded or tipped cats. The group was granted preliminary status in 1992 and Burmilla, Asian Smoke, Asian Tabby, Bombay and Tiffanie are currently recognized. Any kittens showing the Burmese expression in coat are registered as Asian Variants to avoid confusion with true Burmese to which, in phenotype, they are identical.

BENGAL

The Bengal and Snow Bengal form another American breed that has only recently been exported to the United Kingdom. In the early 1960s an Asian Leopard Cat and a domestic shorthair were mated, but it was not until the 1980s that a breeding plan was implemented to produce a cat with a spotted, 'wild cat' pelt, but with the disposition of the domestic. This new breed, now called the Bengal, aroused great interest. While accepted by some American fancies, the Bengal has still to gain preliminary recognition in the United Kingdom.

CORNISH AND DEVON REX

Both the Cornish and the Devon Rex resulted from natural genetic mutations that gave rise to their curly fur. Despite their similarity and origins in south-west England, they are quite distinct breeds. The first Cornish Rex was one of a litter born to a farm cat in 1950. The siblings had straight coats, so the owner sought the local vet's advice and decided to mate this kitten back to its mother. This produced a higher ratio of curly-coated kittens. It was then acknowledged that a new, natural mutation had occurred and a breeding programme was established.

A decade later, another curly-coated kitten was born in Devon. This was mated to a Cornish curly-coated cat, but all the kittens were straight coated, so it was evident that different genes were involved. Cornish and Devon Rexes have held Championship status for many years. Recognized in almost any colour and pattern; their most important credential is the quality of the rexing.

THE EGYPTIAN MAU

An American designed breed, Egyptian Maus should not be confused with Oriental Tabbies, once known by this name in the United Kingdom. Unknown now in Britain, the Egyptian Mau is a spotted cat of modified Oriental/Siamese type. The head is more rounded with a less straight profile than the Siamese. The tail is gently tapering. The eye set is almond shaped but not the 'Oriental' slant; the colour is medium to pale green.

JAPANESE BOBTAIL

As yet unseen in the United Kingdom, this is a popular breed in the United States and its native Japan. It has a vestigial tail, carried upright when the cat is moving, curling gently when it is relaxed. It is muscular and medium-sized but slender and dainty. The head has a medium wedge, largish ears and large, slanting eyes. The restricted coat pattern is seen in many colours, the most popular being Red, Black and Tortoiseshell.

KORAT

An ancient breed from Thailand, it went to the United States in the 1950s and the United Kingdom in 1972. One of the few breeds unchanged by breeding programmes, it has a heart-shaped face, a gently tapering muzzle and large, round, green eyes. The body is firm, compact and muscular; females are dainty, while males are more muscular and cobby. The evenly hued, silver tipped blue coat is sleek with a distinct 'breaking' of the fur along the spine; this is unique to the Korat.

OCICAT

When Virginia Daly was trying to breed a Siamese with Abyssinian 'points', other non-restrictive patterned tabby kittens were produced, one of which has become the spotted breed now known as the Ocicat. Originally, an Abyssinian male was mated to a Seal Point Siamese. A female 'Abyssinian hybrid' was kept and mated to a Chocolate Point Siamese; a spotted kitten was born and this is classified as the first Ocicat. This breed was accepted for Championship status in the United States in 1987, but has only recently been exported to Britain.

THE RUSSIAN BLUE

One of the older Foreign breeds, the Russian Blue was known as the Archangel Cat, after the city in northern Russia. Sweet-natured and intelligent, they are neither so vociferous nor so demanding as some other Foreign varieties. Blue cats are seen in almost every breed, but there are only two true Self Blue Shorthairs that do not have variations in colour: the Russian and the Korat. The standards call for an elegant cat with long, slim legs, longer at the back than the front. Its movement has to be seen to be believed and is unique to this breed.

SCOTTISH FOLD

First seen in a litter of Scottish farm cats in the early 1950s, this breed was so named because its ears are folded forward, giving the cat an almost owl-like expression. Although popular in the United States, it is not recognized by the Governing Council of the Cat Fancy in the United Kingdom because the folded ears are considered unacceptable and could be detrimental to the cat's well-being.

SINGAPURA

Although popular in both the United States and Europe, this friendly, sweet-natured cat has only recently been seen in the United Kingdom, where it is currently one of the rarer of the new breeds. Singapuras have delightful temperaments, their short fur is easy to groom, and if a dainty, petite cat is your preference, this could well be a breed worth considering.

SNOWSHOE

This breed was developed in the 1960s by Dorothy Hinds-Daugherty of Philadelphia, who mated a Siamese with an American Bi-Colour Shorthair. The cat's white paws result from the gene for low-grade white spotting, introduced from the Bi-Colour. It is a solid cat of modified Oriental type, with the restricted Himalayan coat pattern of the Siamese. It is accepted in any of the colours recognized for Siamese, but with white paws.

For perfection, the facial markings, known as the 'burglar's mask', should show an inverted V-shaped area of white extending outwards from between the eyes over and under the chin. It is accepted by some of the American fancies but is quite rare in the United Kingdom, where it is not recognized by the Governing Council of the Cat Fancy.

SPHYNX

Another breed showing a natural mutation of the fur, it was first seen in Canada in 1966. This breed is often described as hairless, but is covered with a very soft layer of downy fur. It is a solid, muscular, broad-chested cat with long, slender legs and a long, whiplike tail. It should have evenly distributed down, which may be denser on the legs and tail. It is a characterful cat, takes life as it comes and is both intelligent and inquisitive.

TONKINESE

This is a Burmese/Siamese cross which, as the first Burmese is thought a hybrid, could claim to be the older breed. In the 1960s, breeders thought to recreate the Tonkinese, as it has all the good points of both varieties without showing the extremes of either. When mated together, there is the possibility that a phenotypically Burmese or Siamese will result; these are registered as Tonkinese Variants to protect the purity of the mainstream breeds. Outgoing and intelligent, they are a good compromise if you prefer the Siamese character in the old-fashioned chunkier Siamese shape.

OPPOSITE: *Although a youngster, this Usual Abyssinian shows the good rich golden brown base coat and even black ticking. The underparts show an excellent ruddy orange colour and the black tail tip is as required.*

BELOW: *All kittens go through a fluffy period as seen in this little Sorrel Abyssinian. Even in a kitten of such a young age the coat colour is showing the required rich shade of copper ticked in chocolate.*

BELOW: *This Sorrel Abyssinian kitten shows excellent ear tufting and the typical alert expression, but there is a little bit too much white around the muzzle for show perfection.*

OPPOSITE: *The Blue Abyssinian is one of the newer colours and is a soft warm blue-grey colour, ticked in deep steel blue. This colour is rapidly gaining popularity.*

PREVIOUS PAGES: *This Usual Somali kitten shows the required colour for this variety but has yet to develop the full coat of the adult (inset), which in maturity gives this breed its typical foxy look.*

ABOVE AND OPPOSITE: *When a shorthaired kitten appears in a Somali litter, although it has the outward appearance of an Abyssinian, it will carry the longhair gene and so is registered under the term Somali Variant. The photograph (opposite) shows an adult Variant with her delightful Somali kitten.*

LEFT AND BELOW: *The Bengal is a sturdy, muscular breed of cat which, despite its wild cat appearance, is reputed to have a delightful temperament. Both these examples show good, clear spotting. The Bengal is reputed to be an excellent example of 'hybrid vigour'. An American geneticist, working on the DNA structure of the Asian Leopard cat, discovered that this species did not have a Feline Leukaemia Virus genome in its genetic make-up and so is immune to this disease. He also carried out research on the Bengal's DNA and found that the genome was not present in this breed either.*

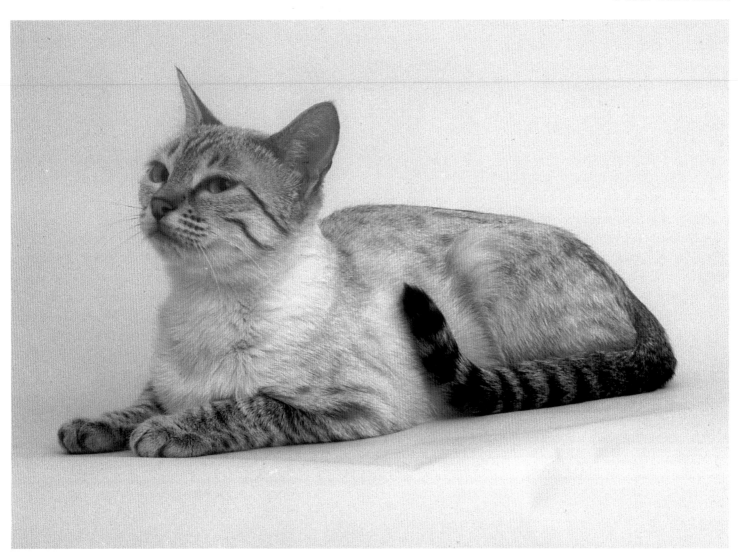

ABOVE AND RIGHT: *The Snow Bengal is the silver version of the Bengal. All these jungle cats love water. The owner of this splendid cat finds a shallow bath of water and a ping pong ball will keep him amused for hours.*

BELOW: *One of the original litter of Burmillas – the result of the accidental mating between a Chinchilla and a Lilac Burmese. The two cats had grown up together and were inseparable. When the Burmese began her first call, her owner decided that it would be sensible to keep the cats apart until she could be taken to her appointed Burmese stud cat. However, the housekeeper, feeling sorry for the lovelorn Chinchilla, opened a door to let the two cats be together. Sixty-five days later, the kittens were born – and the rest is history.*

OPPOSITE: *Several generations later, colours such as this Chocolate Silver Tipped have developed.*

FOLLOWING PAGES: *The term Burmilla applies to those cats within the Asian group that are shaded or tipped. The photographs show a Brown Shaded Silver Burmilla (main picture) and a Brown Tipped Burmilla (inset).*

BELOW AND OPPOSITE: *Asians are bred in a wide variety of colours and patterns. Shown here are an Asian Brown Silver Ticked Tabby (below), and an Asian Smoke (opposite).*

OPPOSITE: *It was realized from the outset of the Asian breeding programme that a broad spectrum of colours may be possible – here is an Apricot Ticked Tabby.*

BELOW: *The longhaired version of the Asian is known as a Tiffanie and this is a fine example of a Cream.*

BOTTOM: *The Self-Black Asian with its characteristic sleek, glossy coat is known as the Bombay.*

PREVIOUS PAGES: *The American Wirehair is a uniquely American breed, the result of a natural mutation. It has a characteristic springy, wiry coat.*

PREVIOUS PAGES, INSET: *The American Curl may be longhaired or shorthaired and of almost any colour or pattern. The most important point is that the large, round-tipped, well-furnished ears should show a distinct curl round towards the back of the head.*

BELOW: *Cornish Rex have extremely outgoing personalities and the kittens in this litter all show the alert expression so typical of this breed. They will enjoy – almost need – plenty of attention and company and are certainly not a breed to select if you enjoy a quiet life! They will become a conversation piece, so do not be tempted to buy one of these if you simply want to show off the cat to friends as some sort of 'novelty'. They may have strange-textured fur, but, like all cats, have their own feelings.*

OPPOSITE: *The adult Cornish Rex should be a well-muscled cat and the coat should have a good covering of well 'rexed' fur all over, as this fine red male neuter displays admirably.*

OPPOSITE AND BELOW: *Cornish Rex are allowed in almost every possible colour and pattern. The most important point is the 'rexing' of the fur. Both the Blue Cream (opposite) and Bi-Colour (below) show this well.*

OPPOSITE, RIGHT AND BELOW: *The Devon Rex is another curly-coated breed but genetically quite separate from the Cornish Rex. They are bred in a wide range of colours, among which are Tortie, (opposite), Cream Tabby (right) and Smoke (below). They are smaller cats than the Cornish Rex with a typical 'pixie' expression that truly reflects this breed's character – mischievous! Over the years they have been called the 'E.T.s' or even the 'Gremlins' of the cat world, as they do have a faintly extra-terrestrial look about them!*

156

Cats

PREVIOUS PAGES: *The Ocicat is a spotted variety of cat that was created in the United States. It should always look heavy and well-muscled and has a strong chest. The hindquarters are slightly higher than the front. The head is a modified wedge with a broad muzzle, strong chin, firm bite and, in profile, the muzzle should show a slight drop from the bridge of the nose to the nose leather. The general size of the cat is large; an adult cat should weight 4.5-6.8 kg (10-15 lb), with the males weighing in even heavier. The coat should be tight and sleek, with the typical, well-scattered spots, circled by smaller spots, most prominent against the background colour. Many background colours are acceptable but any white lockets are a definite fault. The eyes are almond shaped and may be any hue from amber to green, although the density of colour is the most important; blue is most frowned upon and would be a disqualifying point if manifested in an adult Ocicat at a show.*

OPPOSITE: *The Egyptian Mau is an American breed of modified Oriental type. It should not be confused with the Oriental Spotted Tabbies in the United Kingdom which are a completely different breed that were originally given the same name. 'Mau' is the Egyptian for cat, but the name of this breed does not mean that it has an archaeological ancestry; it is purely 'man-made' and cannot lay any claim to having originated in Egypt.*

LEFT: *In Japan the Japanese Bobtail is considered a symbol of good luck and is known there as the Mi-Ke cat. Most Japanese households display a statue or painting of the Mi-Ke as a welcome to visitors.*

RIGHT: *The Scottish Fold first occurred as a natural mutation in Scotland. Unrecognized by the Governing Council of the Cat Fancy in the United Kingdom, it is popular in the United States. The temperament is similar to that of the British and American Shorthairs: gentle, kind and big-hearted.*

OPPOSITE AND BELOW: *The Korat is one of the oldest breeds known and is still one of the few that is seen only in the one original colour – blue. It originated in Thailand, where it is regarded as the sacred cat known as Si-Sawat; this can be translated as 'good fortune' and this breed has always been highly prized in its native country. It is interesting that both Burmese and Korats have yellow eyes in adolescence. The Burmese eyes should stay this colour and green is considered a fault; the opposite is true of Korats, where the yellow phase is considered transient and the true green often takes a couple of years to develop!*

PREVIOUS PAGES: *The Russian Blue is another essentially blue only breed. Although occasional black and white Russians have been noted, a breeding programme has not been pursued. The coat should have a very different feel from that of any other breed; it is a double coat, insulating the cat against severely cold climates, and is short and thick. With its long, slim legs, the Russian's movement is graceful, rather like a ballerina dancing en pointe.*

BELOW: *Native to Singapore, where because of its small size and gutter lifestyle it was known as the 'drain cat', this breed nearly became extinct in its own country. As it was popular in both the United States and Europe, a breeding programme was started to preserve the Singapura and they have recently been exported to England.*

OPPOSITE: *The Snowshoe is another shorthaired breed showing a restricted coat pattern. With its typical white paws, it resembles a Birman, to which it is unrelated. Its origins are, in fact, from the Siamese.*

OPPOSITE: *The Sphynx is one of the rarer breeds of cat and is popularly referred to as the hairless cat. This is a common misconception as, in fact, the Sphynx should be covered with a very thin layer of down-like fur that feels a little like the softest chamois leather.*

RIGHT AND FOLLOWING PAGES: *The Tonkinese is a hybrid of Burmese/Siamese ancestry and is neither so long nor so svelte as the Siamese, nor is it so solidly built as the Burmese. Tonkinese have recently been granted preliminary status by the Governing Council of the Cat Fancy in a variety of colours. These include Chocolate (right), and on the following pages, Cream (inset left), Brown Tortie (inset right) and Lilac (main picture).*

ORIENTALS

The Orientals are essentially Siamese cats but without the restricted Himalayan coat pattern. They are an intelligent breed, with the outgoing personality typical of the Siamese. Orientals do not like to be ignored and prefer to be considered part of a family. They dislike being left alone for any length of time, so if you are out at work all day, get two kittens not just one; a single cat will quickly become bored and may well become destructive. In general, their voices are neither quite so loud nor so demonstrative as those of the Siamese, but they still demand more attention than British or Persian cats.

ORIENTALS

Orientals do not like to live in an overcrowded environment, preferring to have plenty of their own space. Despite their grace and beauty, do not be tempted to keep too many of this breed, as it might just end in tears before bedtime or, more often, a hefty cat fight. Burmese and Siamese are the same in this respect: once a colony of cats 'fall out' with each other, it can be extremely difficult – virtually impossible – to re-integrate them successfully. This is the main reason for cats of these breeds needing to be re-homed. Remember, moderation in all things, especially certain breeds of cats, and do not have too much of a good thing!

HISTORY

The Oriental is a genetically engineered breed of cat that first became popular in the 1950s. Prior to this, solid coloured cats of Siamese type had been seen, but they were usually the result of accidental matings. A structured breeding programme started when a Seal Point Siamese, Tsui Chow, was mated to a solid colour shorthair, recorded simply as a 'fluffy black non-registered cat'. This produced a kitten, registered under the name of Elmtower Susannah, and she paved the way to the breed we now call the Havana, a self-coated brown cat quite distinct from the Brown Burmese. Other out-crosses were employed in this programme, most usually the Russian Blue, but also other Self-Coloured Shorthairs.

In the late 1960s, a spotted tabby version of the Oriental was bred in the United Kingdom. It was given the name Egyptian Mau because of a distinctive 'scarab' marking on its forehead. Later, in 1978, this breed became known in Britain as the Oriental Spotted Tabby and is quite distinct in both type and origin from the breed known in the United States as the Egyptian Mau.

In the same way as the Balinese – a semi-longhaired version of the Siamese – had been developed, so, too, was a semi-longhaired version of the Oriental. This is known as the Angora. It is, however, quite distinct from the early longhaired breed that came from Turkey at the turn of the century and was also known as the Angora, named after the city of Ankara. The modern breed of this name is completely 'breeder designed'.

COLOURS AND PATTERNS

From the earliest days of the breeding programme, kittens of a different hue would appear in litters of Havanas. These were a pale grey colour and became known as the Foreign Lilac. During this time, breeders were experimenting to produce Siamese in many different colours; if it could be done with Siamese, it seemed just as possible that they could create new colours in Orientals.

Other solid colours soon followed – Oriental Blacks, Blues and Whites and the newer colours, such as Cinnamon, Caramel, Fawn, Red and Cream.

Patterned colours of this group include the Oriental Tortie, a sex-linked colour that is usually a female only variety. By mating back to Tabby Point Siamese, a series of Oriental Tabbies became possible: Spotted, Classic and Mackerel. The even-coated Ticked Tabby arrived by mating back to the Abyssinian. The Oriental Tabbies, especially the Spotted and Ticked, are among the most glamorous and popular of this group, reflecting the coat pattern of their distant 'wild cat' ancestors.

Within this group, new colours are constantly being developed. These include Smoke, Shaded, Tipped and the dilute colours of Tortie.

The Angora is recognized in just the same colours and coat patterns as the Oriental.

TYPE AND JUDGING STANDARDS

In general, all the Orientals, with the exceptions of the Foreign White and the Angora, conform to the same standard of points.

This is an elegant breed and should always have a well-balanced, muscular appearance, with long, graceful limbs, a slender neck and a long, whiplike tail that is free from any kink or other defect. The general body conformation is similar to that of the Siamese: long and elegant with a close-lying, fine-textured coat. The exception is the Angora, the semi-longhaired version of the Oriental, which should have a free-flowing, silky coat, comparable with that of the semi-longhaired Siamese, the Balinese.

In profile, the head should show a long straight nose without any sign of a dip or break; from the front, there should be no sign of a muzzle pinch and the head should, for perfection, resemble a triangle from the tips of the wide-set ears to the tip of the muzzle. The eyes are typically Oriental in shape – slanting and with good width between the nose – but should never have any sign of a squint; this is a bad fault. The required eye colour for most coat colours and patterns is a clear green with no flecks of other colours. In the Red and Cream any shade from copper to green is acceptable. The Foreign White should display the brilliant blue eyes of the Siamese.

GOOD POINTS

Friendly and affectionate

Good with most other animals

Easy to groom; the Angora, although it has long fur,

needs much less grooming than a Persian

Elegant and aristocratic appearance

Highly intelligent

BAD POINTS

Can be noisy, especially when 'calling'

Does not like to be left alone and prefers the company

of another feline companion

Tends to be sexually precocious; if you buy kittens of

different sexes, do keep an eye out for sexual activity or

you may become a cat breeder before you had planned

As with Siamese, from which they originated, Orientals

are very territorial and may be more likely to 'spray'

than other breeds

OPPOSITE: *Typically, Orientals exude elegance. This Black is a fine example of the breed, and his looks just shout that he is an aristocratic, pedigree cat: the sleek, glossy, jet black coat solid to the roots, a long lithe body with slim legs, a haughty expression and, for the finishing touch, deep green eyes.*

BELOW: *Whatever the colour or pattern, Orientals are still essentially Siamese wearing a different, unrestricted coat. One of the newer, solid colours is the Cinnamon, a lovely warm cinnamon-brown shade. This was the result of a Siamese to Abyssinian mating in the later 1960s and it was this that introduced the sorrel gene into the Oriental breed. Cinnamon in the Orientals is the genetic colour equivalent of sorrel in Abyssinians; the dilute version is known as Fawn.*

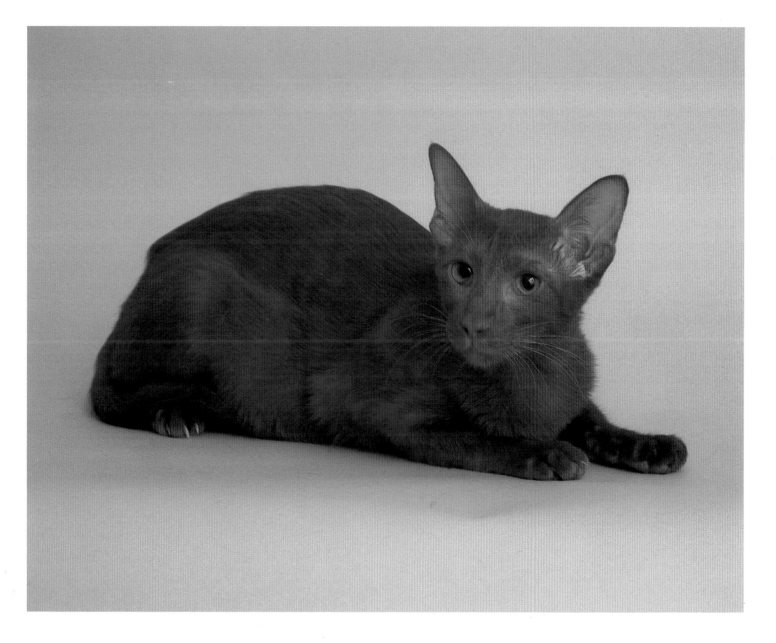

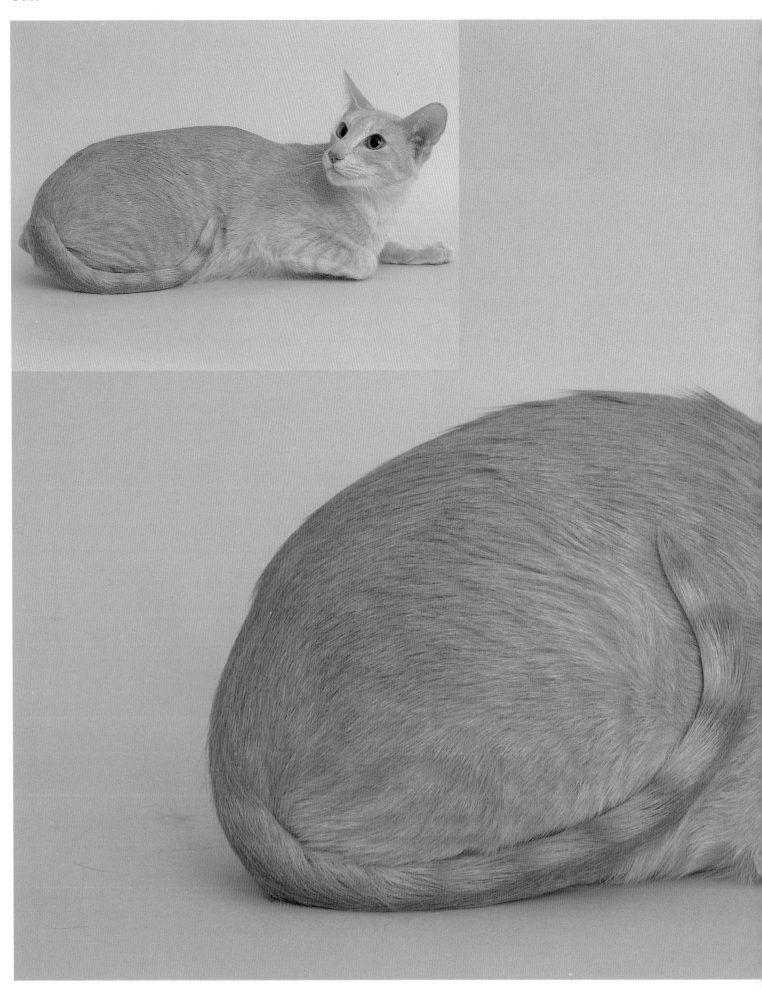

PREVIOUS PAGES: *Cream is one of the sex-linked colours and is the dilute of red. Mated to Caramel, Apricot can appear – a new colour currently pending recognition by the Governing Council of the Cat Fancy in Britain.*

BELOW AND OPPOSITE: *The Havana is probably the best known of the Orientals as it was the result of the original breeding programme designed to produce a cat of Siamese type with a solid coat colour. They are warm*

chestnut-coloured cats, lighter in colour and richer in tone than the Brown Burmese, with which they are sometimes confused (see page 203). As with all Self-Coloured Orientals, the coat should be solid to the roots.

FOLLOWING PAGES: *The Foreign White, with blue eyes, is the only colour in this group without the typical green eyes. Blue-eyed whites are often associated with deafness, but the Oriental White was specifically bred to produce a blue-eyed white cat with perfect hearing. They are not usually mated to other Orientals, but to Seal Point Siamese as this helps to keep the blue eye colour and type.*

OPPOSITE: *Oriental Spotted Tabbies are one of the newer coat patterns of this variety. First seen in the late 1960s they are now one of the most popular of this breed. This Chocolate Spotted Tabby shows beautifully defined warm chocolate brown* *spotting set off against the correct warm bronze base colour. Until 1978 Oriental Spotted Tabbies in Britain were called Egyptian Maus. They are quite different from the cats of the same name that are bred in the United States (see page 160).*

BELOW: *This photograph shows an early Lilac Spotted Tabby, a colour originally known as Lavender. Lilac is the dilute of Chocolate and these dilute colours show less pronounced markings and the spots are not so obvious. The colour of Lilac should not be confused with the new shade known as Caramel, the dilute of which is Apricot.*

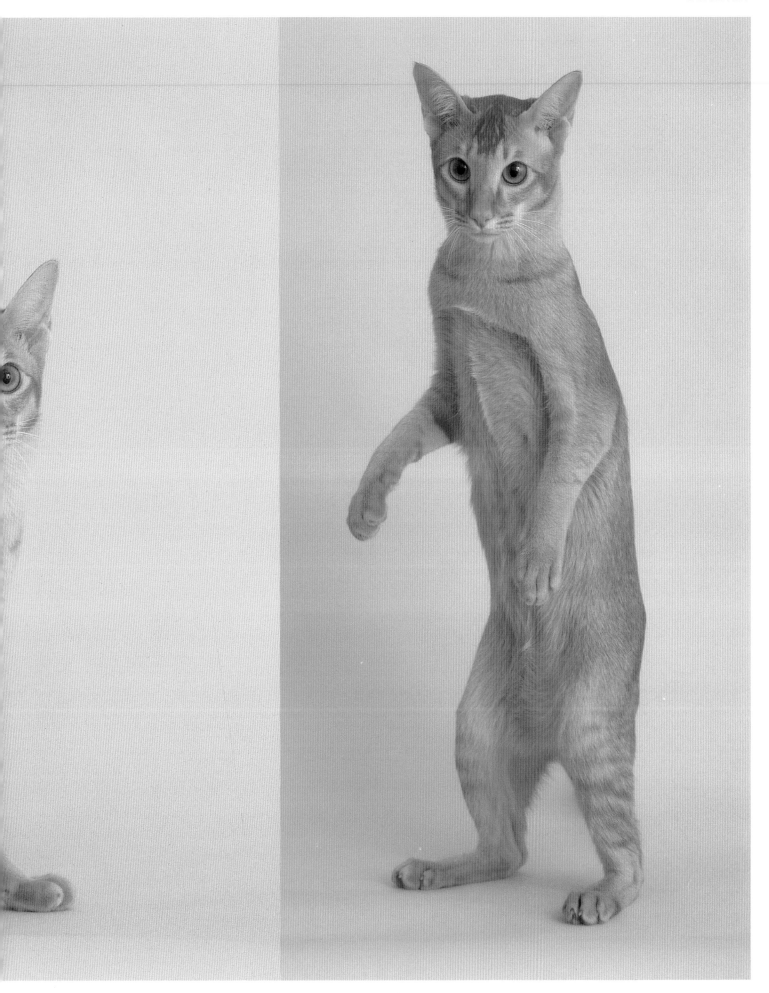

PREVIOUS PAGES: *The Ticked Tabby is another pattern that resulted from the original Siamese/Abyssinian matings. As shown by this Red Ticked Tabby, they have evenly ticked coats, without obvious tabby patterns or markings on the body. In 1993, these Ticked Tabby Orientals were granted championship status in the United Kingdom, with the exception of Fawn and Apricot, but including Silver and Tortoiseshell Ticked among the more obvious colours.*

OPPOSITE: *Cinnamon is the result of a limited gene pool and both parents have to carry the gene for this colour in order for Cinnamon kittens to be produced. Recently, kittens have been exported to and imported from Holland, where Dutch breeders have been developing an independent Cinnamon breeding programme since the late 1960s. This has helped to increase the gene pool and the Cinnamon Ticked Tabby shown here is the offspring of a Dutch Cinnamon kitten exported to Britain from Holland in 1989.*

BELOW: *Lilac Ticked is the dilute of Chocolate. As the result of many ticked to ticked matings, the Ticked Tabby can lose its tabby markings on legs, neck and tail, becoming more similar to the Abyssinian pattern. Also, instead of having the typical 'scarab' marking on the forehead, it shows just a solid skullcap. According to present Governing Council of the Cat Fancy standards, this pattern is not acceptable although cats so marked can still form a useful part of a breeding programme.*

OPPOSITE : *Tortoiseshell cats, of whatever breed, are a female only variety with few exceptions; an occasional male tortie has been seen, but they are usually sterile. However, there is always an exception to prove the rule and a Tortie Point fertile male Siamese has occurred in Australia.*

ABOVE: *This Chocolate Tortoiseshell Ticked Oriental, is the first registered with the Governing Council of the Cat Fancy. The tortie markings are masked by the tabby pattern, which is considered more important. This variety is seen in as many recognized colours as torties in general.*

BELOW: *Angoras are the longhaired version of Orientals. It is thought that the longhaired gene came through the early mating with Abyssinians, many of which carried the longhaired gene that produced the Somalis. They are recognized in all the colours accepted for Orientals in general.*

RIGHT AND OPPOSITE BOTTOM: *This photograph shows an Oriental Classic Silver Tabby. The silver gene was introduced to the Orientals in the early 1970s from a mating between a Chinchilla Persian and a Chocolate Point Siamese. A breeding programme began whereby the inhibitor gene was introduced. This produced Silvers, Shadeds and Smokes.*

RIGHT BOTTOM: *Another example of the silver series, this Silver Spotted shows the required round, evenly distributed spots with no sign of a striped pattern.*

OPPOSITE TOP: *The Black Smoke has a near-white undercoat that is not at first apparent. This pale coloration should form approximately one-third of the shaft of each hair.*

BURMESE

Burmese have extremely outgoing personalities, have minds of their own and are not afraid to express their opinions. This could take the form of rearranging your home to suit their own needs and comforts; they like sitting in high places, so it is inadvisable to have ornaments on a surface that could be construed as a launching pad! If they are ignored, they will be quite vocal in expressing their disapproval. They are insistent, extremely playful and both demand and need human attention. They are extremely stubborn when they want to play and you do not; a toy will be dropped at your feet or on your papers until you have to give up what you are doing and join in a Burmese game.

B U R M E S E

For those who like this breed, the previous page explains a very large part of their charm; others may feel that Burmese are one of the most annoying breeds ever born. If you are contemplating a Burmese for yourself, it is a good idea to visit an already Burmese populated home. This will give you far and away the best idea of how these cats behave in a domestic environment – and how powerfully one in your own home could change your life!

However, for all their demands, they will reward you with undying love and almost dog-like devotion. They are cats that really need people around them. They also enjoy feline company, but do not like overcrowding. Their sweet natures can easily lead you to fall into the trap of keeping another and another and... until it comes to the point where they fall out with each other, leading to cat fights and the very anti-social (to humans) feline habit of territorial urine spraying. These are the main reasons for Burmese being re-homed and would not be necessary if one simple rule were followed – moderation in all things, especially Burmese cats.

Simply, Burmese are not for the faint-hearted. They will try your patience. They will expect to be treated not just as 'pet cats', but as members of the family. They lay down the rules and you obey. Their logic is quite simple: they think – perhaps know – that they are infinitely superior to humans.

HISTORY

Burmese cats are relative newcomers to the cat world as they were only introduced towards the middle of this century, but now they are probably more popular than Siamese. They may not have the glamorous coat pattern of the Siamese, nor look so obviously pedigree; it is their charming characters, intelligence and 'naughty but nice' temperaments that have made them so popular.

It is generally accepted that the Burmese breed originated from Wong Mau, affectionately referred to as 'little brown cat'. She was a brown female brought from the Far East to the west coast of the United States by Dr. Thompson in 1930. As, at the time, there were no other brown cats in America, she was mated to a cat of the breed that most closely resembled her – a Siamese. The resulting kittens were obviously hybrids and it is reasonably likely that Wong Mau herself was a hybrid, too. However, when one of her sons was mated back to her, some of the kittens were brown like her and this is the point where the Burmese breed officially began. The British were a little slower, and it was not until 1948 that the first Burmese were imported into the United Kingdom.

Legend tells that Burmese were the sacred cats appointed to guard Buddhist temples, but the Semi-Longhair Birmans (see Chapter 2) stake the same claim. Who can say which one is right? Frankly, I doubt that a Burmese would be content to spend its days working as a kind of religious security officer!

COLOURS AND PATTERNS –
HOW THEY DEVELOPED

As the early Burmese had Siamese in their pedigrees, it was not long before colours other than Brown, known as Sable in the United States, were to be seen. Kittens of the dilute colours of Champagne and Platinum were born in the United States. However, it was not until 1969-70 that these colours were imported into Britain, where they are known as Chocolate and Lilac, respectively. Meanwhile, in England, in 1955, a Blue Burmese was born and, with great imagination, was called Blue Surprise! These four colours – Brown, Blue, Chocolate and Lilac – are the genetic equivalent of Seal, Blue, Chocolate and Lilac Points in Siamese.

As a result of the dedicated work started by two British breeders between 1965 and 1975, another spectrum of colours became possible – the Red, Cream and Tortie series. Cream is the dilute of Red and there are now Brown, Blue, Chocolate and Lilac Torties.

In the United States, there is a semi-longhaired version of the Burmese, called the Tiffany and a Burmese-related self-black, known as the Bombay. In the United Kingdom, these are classified under the Asian-Burmilla group and the semi-longhair (spelled Tiffanie in Britain) is recognized in all the Asian colours and patterns as well as those accepted for Burmese (see pages 142-9, Asian-Burmilla group).

TYPE AND JUDGING STANDARDS

The Burmese is a compact, well-muscled cat of medium size. It is neither as large as the British nor as slender as the Siamese and should feel heavier than its appearance suggests. The legs are slender, with the hind legs slightly longer than the front ones. The tail is long but not whiplike, as in the Siamese, nor thick, as in the British. It should be in proportion to the body length and should typically end in a 'paint brush' tip. The head should be a rounded dome with a good width between the medium-sized ears, which should not show tufted tips. The cheekbones are wide, tapering to a short, blunt wedge. The almond-shaped eyes should be a golden yellow, but the colour may vary from amber to yellow chartreuse; a slight greenish tinge is acceptable but any trace of blue is considered a fault. In profile, the head should show a definite nose break, and a strong, firm chin. Whatever the coat colour, it should be clear of any markings or bars.

GOOD POINTS

Highly intelligent

Short coats that do not need much grooming

Friendly and sociable

Generally, an adaptable breed; if you are a two-home
family, Burmese seem to adjust just as well to weekday
city life as to weekend country life

Companionable – Burmese tend to sense your moods
and feelings

Burmese have a sense of humour, but only at your
expense; never laugh at a Burmese

As one owner sums them up 'Burmese don't have
brains, they have a craftiness'

BAD POINTS

Naughty (especially the torties)

Can be noisy, especially when calling; but not so noisy
as Siamese

Territorial – will fight strange cats and may be prone
to spraying their territory

Need their own space – Burmese may be beautiful but
do not be persuaded to keep too many unless you have
a very large house

Overcrowded Burmese tend to fall out with each
other, resulting in cat fights

They may walk with grace and elegance, but they can
be dreadfully clumsy; keep valuable ornaments out of
reach

They are inquisitive and have no fear; keep them
away from cars and other dangers

PREVIOUS PAGES: *This is an example of an older-type Burmese, but this cat still shows the strong, muscular body that is so desired in this breed. The facial profile shows a good nose break and a firm chin.*

PREVIOUS PAGE, INSET: *This Brown Burmese, with a beautiful, even, glossy coat, shows really excellent head type. He displays a fine, medium round head, with good breadth between the ears and a rounded dome. The eyes are a lovely shape and set. Altogether, this makes for the typical alert Burmese expression – just what the judge has ordered!*

LEFT AND OPPOSITE: *Burmese are not self-coloured cats, in that the kittens are not born the colour that they will display in maturity. The Chocolate kitten (left) shows a pale coloration that will develop into the required even, warm chocolate colour so desired in the adult (opposite).*

PREVIOUS PAGES, LEFT AND OPPOSITE: *Blue Burmese should have an even, medium blue coat with a silver sheen – they should never be too dark or too light. The kitten (left) shows the typical 'fluffy' coat which will smooth out as she grows older. The female (opposite) has a superb profile and fine eye colour but is noticeably more feminine and finely boned than the gorgeous Blue male neuter (previous pages) who has just the correct shade of colour. A large, muscular cat, his expression reflects the typically sweet, if sometimes mischievous, Burmese temperament.*

BELOW AND OPPOSITE: *The desired coat colour of Lilac (Platinum in the United States) Burmese is a pale dove grey with a pinkish tinge, as these three cats all admirably display. The family resemblance in this Grand Champion mother and daughter portrait (below) is quite unmistakable, while the unrelated Champion and Grand Premier neuter male (opposite) shows a wonderfully even, pale coat.*

PREVIOUS PAGES: *Red and Cream Burmese are among the newer, sex-linked colours, which includes the Tortie series. The Reds (main picture) in maturity have a rich tangerine colour, while the kitten (inset) will have a paler hue until it matures.*

LEFT AND OPPOSITE: *The Cream youngster (opposite) has the required warm cream coloration, with a 'powdery' touch that makes it look as if it has been lightly dusted with talcum. The Grand Champion male (left) really shows the muscular elegance so desired in this breed.*

PREVIOUS PAGES, OPPOSITE, BELOW AND FOLLOWING PAGES: *Whatever the colour of Tortie, the type should be typical Burmese and the combination of colours should be well mingled, never showing tabby markings or any sign of white. The Brown Torties (previous pages) both show different, but correct mixtures of brown and red. The Blue Tortie (opposite) is a mixture of blue and cream while the Chocolate Tortie (below) is a mixture of chocolate and red, as is the one on the following pages.*

BELOW & RIGHT:
Lilac Tortie Burmese showing a well mingled mixture of lilac and cream. (Below) shows an excellent nose break while (Right) shows a good depth of eye colour.

FOLLOWING PAGES:-
Burmese may be known for having large litters, but this spectacular collection of 12 kittens is actually two separate litters who grew up together. The colours that can be seen between them are Brown, Blue, Chocolate and Lilac. Insets: Chocolate Burmese

SIAMESE

Siamese are one of the oldest and best known of all the pedigree breeds. They are elegant cats – long, lithe and muscular, and their distinctive coloured points, set off against a pale body colour, give them a most aristocratic appearance.

They are highly intelligent but can be rather demanding. They do like plenty of attention and love to play games involving their owner, especially 'retrieving' screwed up pieces of paper! They are also extremely vocal; to lovers of this breed, their idiosyncratic voice is part of their charm, but to others it is most annoying and can be likened to a baby's cry.

S I A M E S E

Siamese enjoy the company of other cats but usually get on best with other Siamese or another strong-willed breed, such as Burmese; they do tend to be rather bossy, and one of the quieter breeds, such as Persians, would not get much peace in a Siamese-dominated household.

They have a real need for human companionship and will become devoted to their owners. As with all the 'foreign' type cats, they do not like being left on their own for any great length of time and so are not best suited to a home where the owners are out at work all day unless there is another cat for company.

A lonely, bored Siamese is quite likely to become destructive through frustration, just as a small child would if left on its own for several hours. While Siamese enjoy feline company, they do not like to be overcrowded. They are very territorial and if they do not have their own space, they are more likely than most breeds to start spraying – a habit that is extremely hard to break and which is one reason for cats of this breed needing to be re-homed.

HISTORY

Pale, milky coloured cats, with dark seal brown faces, legs and tails, have been known in the
Far East for centuries where they were known as the 'Royal Cat of Siam'. However, it was not until the late 1800s that these Siamese were brought to Europe. In their native country they were highly prized and anyone caught stealing one from the Royal Court of Siam would be punished by death.

However, they were also bestowed on visitors who had found favour with the king, and so eventually made their way to the West, where they are now one of the most popular of pedigree breeds.

The early Siamese tended to have squint eyes and kinked tails. These traits, which have been selectively bred out of the modern Siamese as they are considered faults, have given rise to various legends. They are reputed to have guarded the Buddhist temples and one day a priceless goblet went missing. A pair of Siamese cats were sent off into the jungle to find it and when it was discovered, the female cat stayed to guard it while her partner set off back home for help. She was so worried that the goblet would be stolen again that she never took her eyes off it for a second, and carefully curled her tail around its stem. When her partner returned, he found not only that her eyes squinted and her tail was kinked, but that she had given birth to a litter of squinty-eyed, kinky-tailed kittens. What a price to pay for such devotion to duty!

Another, not quite so romantic story tells of a princess who entrusted her Siamese cat to guard her precious rings while she slept. She placed the rings on the cat's tail but, one night, the cat fell asleep on duty and all the rings fell off and were lost forever. The Princess was not pleased and so tied a knot in the cat's long, slender tail so that this would never happen again! (Ouch!)

COLOURS AND PATTERNS

The original Siamese was the colour we now refer to as Seal Point. Paler coloured kittens were sometimes seen, but these were thought of as poorly coloured and tended to be brushed aside as the richer coloured Seal Point was preferred; these were what we now call the Blue Point. As early as the 1890s other colours were noted, but it was not until 1936 that the Governing Council of the Cat Fancy officially granted recognition to any colour other than Seal and the Blue Point was allowed a breed number of its own. Recognition for the Chocolate Point followed in 1950 and for the Lilac Point in 1960. The latter was accepted in the United States in the mid-1950s, where it is known as Frost Point. Over the years, many other colours and patterns have emerged and Siamese are now recognized in Seal, Blue, Chocolate, Lilac, Red, Cream, Tortie, Tabby and Tortie Tabby Points. Newer colours, such as Cinnamon and Caramel, and their respective dilutes, Fawn and Apricot, have been bred in the United Kingdom, where they are currently pending recognition by the Governing Council of the Cat Fancy. The Semi-Longhair version of the Siamese, the Balinese, was first seen in the United States where it was given official recognition in 1963. It was recognized in Britain by the Governing Council of the Cat Fancy in the early 1980s. Balinese are accepted in all the colours and patterns allowed for Siamese.

TYPE AND JUDGING STANDARDS

The Siamese is essentially an elegant cat – long, slim
and lithe but with a definite muscular feel. The svelte
body is of medium size, the legs long and slim, and the
tail long and whiplike. The head, in profile, should be
long and straight, without any sign of a dip or break.
The ears are large and set low and wide on the head.
The face tapers to a fine muzzle and, when
viewed from the front, the impression is that of a
triangle. The eyes have the typical Oriental slant and
should be of a clear, brilliant blue hue. The darker
'points' should be restricted to the mask, ears, feet and
tail only and show a good contrast from the paler, but
complementary body colour.

Good Points

An elegant, most attractive breed

Short coat that does not require more than routine

grooming

Very sociable

Highly intelligent

Very much 'people' cats and will often become seriously

devoted to their owner

Quite happy to be trained to a harness and lead

for walks

Bad Points

Demanding, and extremely vocal of their needs

Do not like being left alone

More prone to spraying than some other breeds

OPPOSITE: *Seal Point is the original colour of Siamese and this cat sums up all that is required of this breed. The standards call for the Siamese head to be set upon a long and elegant neck and this handsome young male really shows this elegance off to advantage. The colour contrast between the dark points and pale body are very good and the brilliant blue eyes are just the right hue and intensity.*

BELOW: *Whatever the colour of the points, Siamese should have a wedge-shaped face that, when viewed full on, gives the appearance of a triangle from ear tips to nose. This Blue Point displays these features beautifully.*

LEFT: *The overall impression of a Siamese should be elegant but muscular. The Blue Point should have a glacial white body with cool blue markings, as this cat well illustrates.*

OPPOSITE, TOP: *Lilac Points, a dilute of Blue, have a typical pinkish grey tinge to their points.*

OPPOSITE, BOTTOM: *This is an older style Chocolate Point, showing a more 'cobby' appearance. The head shape is not so long as the standards require today, but the contrast between the points is clearly defined and the colour shows the correct milk chocolate.*

PREVIOUS PAGES: *The Red Point Siamese is one of the sex-linked colours and should show bright, reddish gold points. This is an excellent example, and is both a Supreme Grand Champion and a United Kingdom Grand Premier.*

BELOW AND OPPOSITE: *Cream is the dilute of Red and is a pale cream colour that is not so warm a hue as the Red. The cat opposite shows the typical Siamese straight profile.*

PREVIOUS PAGES: *Tortie Points can be Seal, Blue, Chocolate or Lilac and the inset picture shows a well-marked Seal Tortie with typical Siamese expression. As with all tortie cats, they are usually a female only variety; it is rare to find a male tortie. These are normally sterile, although a fertile male Tortie Siamese was recorded in Australia.*

OPPOSITE AND BELOW: *The Tabby Point, known as the Lynx Point in the United States, was recognized as recently as 1966 in the United Kingdom, and is now one of the most popular of all Siamese. It is bred in the same colours as the solid colours, that is Seal, Blue, Chocolate and Lilac.*

OPPOSITE AND RIGHT: *Whatever the colour of Tabby Points, this breed still shows typical Siamese shape, elegance and restricted coat pattern.*

FOLLOWING PAGES: *Balinese are Siamese wearing longer coats. They do require more grooming, but not so much as a full Persian. They have all the same characteristics and playfulness of the Siamese, and are bred in just as many colours.*

PAGES 248-9: *These three neuter males, (main picture) left to right Seal, Red and Blue, all show superb type, excellent eye colour and the correct distribution of colour. It is no wonder that they are all able to add the title of Premier before their names. The inset photographs show a Tabby Point (left) and a Red Point (right).*

A CLOWDER OF KITTENS

Semi-Longhairs

British, European & American Shorthairs

Other ShortHairs

Burmese

Siamese